The Rel

Disc

A spiritual autobiography

Victoria Neville

Kingdom Publishers

www.kingdompublishers.co.uk

The Reluctant Disciple

All Scripture Quotations have been taken from the Interlinear Version of the Bible

ISBN: 978-1-911697-79-4

1st Edition by Kingdom Publishers
Kingdom Publishers
London, UK.

You can purchase copies of this book from any leading bookstore or email
contact@kingdompublishers.co.uk

Dedication

I dedicate this book to my children and my sister Bella and in memory of my sister Henrietta, my beloved father, and Oliver.

Disclaimer

All names in this book have been changed. With
thanks to Ivan Baranasic, Pastor Nigel Lazarus,
Rebecca Colby and Sarah Stanley who have permitted
material to be used in this book, and with much
love and thanks to Laura for all her support and
encouragement.

FOREWORD

Victoria's heart burns with love and passion for Jesus.

It has been an absolute joy and pleasure to journey with her over the past few years and watch her grow in her Christian faith and supernatural anointing, witnessing with my own eyes the transformational and healing presence of God working through her in a powerful way.

I particularly remember the still small whisper in my ear of "look after this one" as we chatted and laughed over pots of tea and biscuits at an event our team delivered in 2021. Over the ensuing months, a deep friendship developed and a ministry partnership that only the Lord himself could have orchestrated.

"Two people are better off than one, for they can help each other succeed"
Ecclesiastes 4:9

God's timing is always perfect, and He knows exactly what we need and when we need it. Over the past few years, the Lord has been steadily growing my trust and dependency on Him and moving me as an evangelist into ministry using the gift of healing and miracles.

I know that our meeting was planned and purposed for His Kingdom glory, and I thank God for bringing us together *for such a time as this.*

In the book of Matthew, Chapter 10, Jesus gave his disciples a mandate to preach the Gospel, heal the sick, cleanse the lepers, raise the dead and cast out devils.

The same mandate applies to all followers of Jesus today.

Victoria has had an extraordinary journey to faith. She is a wonderful storyteller of how Jesus has transformed not only her life, but the lives of many others He has put in her path.

And so, with a grateful heart and fulness of joy, I want to thank God for Victoria, and as we continue on this exciting journey of friendship and ministry, may we both press into what Heaven has stored up for us and unequivocally believe that *"the best is yet to come"*.

Maranatha, Come Lord Jesus.

With gratitude and admiration,

Laura Brett

Victoria has a dynamic, trusting and 'simple' Christian faith. Something much prized by the Lord God of all. Jesus told us we must have 'faith like a little child' in Matt 18.2. Because of this trust in the Lord and His presence in her life by His Holy Spirit, He has been able to enact some amazing acts of healing, deliverance and change. Like the early Christian Apostles, Victoria has heard that God heals, she believes it, and so she sees Him doing it again in our day! For her this is normal Christian life. This book is the story of her life. As one who has gone through many difficulties, she KNOWS that God is good, He is near and He loves her with a passion. Following his command to 'go and make disciples of all nations' is for her the obvious natural response! This is an extremely encouraging read, I thoroughly recommend it.

Rev Richard Fothergill
(Founder of the Filling Station Network)

This book is a wonderful testimony of Victoria exploring her steps of faith in her ministry for Jesus Christ. She shows that having a heart and faith like a child can open doors to the Divine, and enables a believing Christian to operate in the Gifts of the Holy Spirit. Victoria lets nothing stand in her way of showing the love of Messiah Jesus to a hurting world, and she knows that, with his help, she can make a difference. Her street ministry operating in these gifts has changed lives and shows the love of God to all.

This book is a straightforward approach to exercising your faith, street ministry, ministry online, and within church meetings. Spiritual exercising of your faith to wherever the Holy Spirit sees a need. Victoria is growing in her faith and I am excitingly waiting to see where the Lord is going to lead her next. Onwards Victoria. Be Blessed.

Rev Thomas Lewis Griffith

Am so proud of my special friend Victoria for writing this book. She is a true Christian in every sense. I have learnt so much from Victoria and the joy of Jesus shines out of every fibre of her being. Unlike many of us, she will never let an opportunity pass in sharing her faith, so that others can be saved and experience the joy of being a child of Christ.

Lara Fawcett

CEO PR First

Victoria Neville

Contents

Chapter 1

Early Childhood and Out of Body Experience

Everyone has a story to tell, don't they? Usually, those who write Christian books are academics, theologians, those who lead worldwide ministries and are well-known celebrities on television and in the media. I am none of those things. I am in my fifties, and I have been a housewife for most of my adult life, although I did work in the care industry for several years. In other words, I have led a very ordinary life so you might wonder why on earth should I even attempt to write a book in the first place. Surely, I would have nothing to write about. This is the story of how I overcame a miserable childhood, was broken by divorce at the age of 43 but was baptised by the Holy Spirit and set on fire to pray for healing for the sick and the oppressed three years later. I have been in ministry for the last three years and have seen many healed, delivered and also baptised through the power of the Holy Spirit. This book contains testimonies of healing, deliverance and baptisms of the Holy Spirit that I have witnessed first-hand which I want to share, because we overcome by the blood of the lamb and the word of our testimony.

So, let's start at the beginning. I was born in 1970. My start was not promising to say the least. I was the elder of girl twins and my mother had been very unwell during her pregnancy so I was born two and a half months premature and was in intensive care for months before we were allowed home. My mother gave birth interestingly enough at Saint Theresa's hospital in London and the doctors were convinced that my twin and I would not make it. We were named immediately, Victoria and Arabella but we were not given a middle name as we were so premature. We were placed in intensive care in incubators for months. I was born into an aristocratic family and I was christened a few days after my first birthday due to my very premature birth. My father was an Honourable, the son of a Lord and my mother was a very beautiful socialite from Australia. She had been sent to England by her parents to do the season and she had gone skiing in Switzerland with my father and a group of other twenty somethings. During their holiday they fell in love and the rest is history. My father was very good-looking and dashing. He was an English eccentric and when he wasn't working in his office he flew a Cessna, drove very fast on his motorbikes and built a miniature railway in the woods below his house. I spent many years of my childhood watching my father don his boiler suit and drive diesel and electric miniature trains coupled with carriages filled with ecstatic children and their parents every weekend during the summer months. It is running still and is a very well-known tourist attraction in the South of England.

My sisters and I (I had three elder sisters) should have had a very happy child hood. What I didn't know however was that my mother was under immense pressure to have a son to carry on my grandfather's title. My twin Bella and I were my mother's last-ditch attempt to have a son. My mother was 38 when she gave birth to me and my twin so it was too much for her to have any more children and she hit the bottle. My earliest memories therefore instead of being filled with great happiness are tinged with sadness because my father divorced my mother and married my nanny when I was four years old. I did not fully understand what had happened at the time but I knew deep down even though I was only four that all was not well. Interestingly enough I was hospitalised with severe gastro-enteritis at the time of my father's remarriage which I don't think was a coincidence.

Up until the age of five, my twin and I had to go for tests at Great Ormond Street hospital to check that we were developing properly. Fortunately for me, my brain was not damaged in any way by my extremely premature birth but my twin was not so lucky and was diagnosed with learning difficulties, brain damage and dyslexia. I have always felt rather guilty that I should be the one that was unharmed whilst my twin was brain damaged and indeed went on to develop severe epilepsy at the age of thirteen. My mother drank very hard after her divorce and for several years we went to live with my father until my mother was well enough and had stopped drinking. My very first memory is of being five years old and I remember it very clearly. I was at my father's house and my new stepmother was there having tea beside the swimming pool with her parents. I turned around and said to her, "I am going swimming!" and I marched off to the pool house to put my swimming costume on. My stepmother made absolutely no effort to put armbands on me and I jumped straight into the shallow end quick as a flash. Needless to say, I sank straight to the bottom. By the grace of God my father just happened to be walking through the gate, saw it all happen, jumped in and saved my life. The most extraordinary thing is that I literally came out of my body before my father jumped in and pulled me out. I saw my stepmother standing on the edge of the pool with her parents and then I saw my father come running through the gate and jump into the swimming pool. But I never told my father that I came out of my body as he would not have believed me. It was definitely an out-of-body experience, my first spiritual experience and it is one of my earliest memories. Although I was completely unaware of it, God`s hand of protection was over me. My father could easily not have come through the garden gate when he did, just as his hand of protection had brought me through my premature birth. I never did like my stepmother after that. When I was 5, she gave birth to my eldest half-sister and she made it very clear that she did not enjoy having us stay and very much made us feel like second-class citizens. My father was blissfully happy but we were not, and I really hated all the toing and froing between parents, not least because it was a five-hour journey and I was invariably carsick either on the way to my mother's house or on the way back, if not both journeys.

Chapter 2

Angelic Visitation

At the age of eight, I was sent to the local school in Saffron Walden for a term but my stepmother who now had a 2-year-old did not want to have to look after my twin and I so we were soon despatched to Riddlesworth Hall in Norfolk, which was a private girls boarding school from the ages of seven to twelve years of age. We were allowed to take a rabbit or a guinea pig to school which many girls did, to Pets Corner. I remember having great fun climbing trees and playing in the woods on the grounds of the school. The school itself comprised a rather imposing building, constructed in the Victorian era and it was still run I think as a Victorian boarding school would have been run in those days.

There were four houses named after four famous Victorian women. My house was Fry, named after Elizabeth Fry who lived from 1780 to 1845 and was a prison reformer, a social reformer and a philanthropist. She was a major driving force behind new legislation to improve the treatment of prisoners, especially female inmates, and her nickname was the "Angel of Prisons". Another of the houses was named after the famous Victorian nurses Florence Nightingale and Edith Cavell. What I remember most is that if we were caught chatting after lights out, the matron would come in, haul us out of bed and we would be made to stand with our noses to the wall for an hour or march up and down the main corridor and main stairs fifty times which meant the next day you would be completely exhausted and not able to concentrate fully in lessons. I was often chatting after lights out so was hauled out of bed more times than I care to remember!! I also remember the school had all the original huge Victorian baths of which there were not enough to go around so we had to strip wash several nights a week which was fine in the summer but in the winter, it was absolutely freezing as the central heating was fairly minimal and there was absolutely no double glazing anywhere in the entire school.

My twin sadly was kept down two years below me due to her learning difficulties, she should really have gone to a special needs school as the school was totally ill-equipped to teach a child like her with epilepsy and learning difficulties. I, fortunately, was able to keep up with my classmates and was delighted to be away from my stepmother and thoroughly enjoyed making new friends and spent many happy days climbing trees and playing in the woods at the weekends. I am very grateful to my father for sending me there as it gave me a good grounding and exposed me to Christianity. My parents took me to church on Easter and Christmas Day but it was at school that the gospel was explained to me, and where I learnt that it was important to pray. My father was a Christian and went to church every Sunday but I never saw either of my parents pray and I certainly never saw them read the bible. My mother very sadly lost her faith completely after her divorce and never regained it until shortly before she died many years later. However, my mother did buy me a ladybird book when I was 8 years old on the conversion of Saul on the road to Damascus which I still remember even now. It really captured my imagination as it contained colourful vivid pictures of Saul crouching on the road dazzled by a blinding light. I was absolutely captivated by the book and longed to have a similarly breath-taking conversion. Little did I know that years later, Jesus would answer my child-like prayer of faith.

When I was ten years old my father bought a double-decker bus from London as he now had seven daughters so he decided, as only my father would, to buy a double decker bus. He ripped out all the top seats and put beds in and I remember going on a camping holiday to Devon with my father. My elder sisters were 18, 16 and 15 at the time and hated going to campsites so the bus only lasted one summer and was then put out to grass serving teas at the railway. It was also that year that tragedy struck my family as my elder sister who was 15 was killed in a riding accident. My mother had just bought her a new horse which the seller had promised was safe on the roads, and on its first outing a lorry drove too fast and too close to my sister's horse, the horse reared up and my sister fell off. Her hat came off as it was 1980 before riding hats were made with proper chin straps and my sister smashed her head on the road. She was rushed to the hospital and put on a life support machine which my poor mother had to turn off several days later. Not surprisingly the tragedy of losing her daughter so suddenly coupled with her divorce caused my mother to lose all faith in Jesus Christ from that point on. It was however around this time that my second supernatural experience happened in my life.

I was in my dormitory at boarding school in the bottom bunk nearest the window and the moonlight was streaming in as the curtains were rather inadequate, to say the least. For once I didn't feel like chatting with everyone as I was feeling tired that night. There was a child in the next door bed to me and for some reason, I decided to turn round and look at her. I turned to look and all of a sudden, I saw an incandescent figure glowing in the dark kneeling and praying by her bedside. I knew instantly I was seeing a being from another realm and I presumed it must have been her guardian angel. It wasn't a ghost as it was praying and looked very peaceful. Seeing this apparition however scared the living daylights out of me as I had never seen anything like that before and so I started screaming. The figure was there for five minutes and then floated up out of the window. Everyone asked me what the matter was and why I was screaming. I explained what I had seen but mysteriously I was the only person who had seen the angel in the room that night. It was not long after my sister had died and I had been feeling totally grief-stricken. In those days children were not really offered any type of counselling and the pastoral care at my school was practically non-existent. I believe God was trying to comfort me after my sister`s death and he was showing me that although I felt alone, I wasn't as he was upholding me. He was saying to me the words of the poem Footsteps,

"My precious, precious child, I love you and I would never leave you during your time of trial and suffering. When you saw only one set of footprints, it was then that I carried you."

I left Riddlesworth Hall at the age of 12 and moved to St Mary's School Calne. The Headmistress at the time was called Mrs Walters and I remember her as being very strict with a 1940's hairdo and bright red lipstick. She dressed immaculately in crisp white shirts, pencil skirts and very high heels. I hated the school uniform which was dark grey with blue shirts, as I have always thought dark grey to be a depressing colour and rather matched my home life. My twin and I were living with my mother full time by this time with short visits to see my father in the holidays. Bella was diagnosed with epilepsy at the time and she deteriorated and started having grand mal seizures which were very upsetting for her but also difficult for the whole family. My mother was at work in the holidays so I was left alone to care for my twin during the day and often had to make emergency calls to my mother and to ambulances if my twin had an epileptic fit. My mother made a disastrous second marriage to a recovering alcoholic which did not last long. She then remarried for the third time and decided to move out to Spain when I was in the sixth form.

It was in Spain that I had another near-drowning incident. For two years my mother lived out in Spain with my stepfather on the coast near the town of Valencia. One sunny day we were out swimming very far out at sea when the yellow flag was up. All of a sudden, the weather changed and it suddenly became windy and the red flag went up which meant it was a rip tide and it was not safe to swim anymore. My mother and my step-father headed straight back to shore but my twin who was epileptic was terrified and screaming and I was very concerned she might have a fit and drown. So, I swam over to her and towed her all the way back. Unfortunately, my strength ran out before I was able to get to shore and the waves were crashing over Bella and me. I started to panic as I couldn't stand on the sea floor as it was too deep. I then prayed,

"Lord, please send someone to help me and Bella."

Fortunately, a French man who was standing on the beach saw I was in trouble and carried my twin and me to shore as I had no strength left. We were lucky, the same thing happened to a family the following day and all of them were taken to hospital. I never knew if they survived or not. Not surprisingly all of this affected my schooling which is why I scraped through my O levels and my A levels. After my A levels, I went to London to study for a few years where I achieved a BA in English and French. I then stayed in London, found work as a secretary for several years, and met a young lawyer. We were married by the time I was almost 25 and I moved to Yorkshire. Life was beginning to look up at long last!!

Chapter 3

Baptised In Water and By the Holy Spirit

I was thrilled to move to Yorkshire. It seemed like a new chapter of my life was starting. I was happy for the first time in years and I gave birth to my first child at the age of 30. It was shortly after that the most extraordinary thing happened. I was a Christian at the time but not born again as I am now. Anyway, not long after my 30th birthday, my father decided to have a clear-out and he found my baptism card and sent it to me. I was completely astounded that my Father would have kept it after all these years and I read the inscription on it which said that anyone who believes in God and is baptised will be saved and go to heaven. That scripture rather hit me between the eyes and I decided from that moment onwards that I wanted my children to grow up Christians and I started going to church regularly. I started going to prayer groups and reading as many Christian books as I could get my hands on. Sadly, my husband didn't share my faith, and couldn't understand my newfound excitement. Sadly, we started to have frequent rows and steadily grew apart and by 2013 my marriage was completely on the rocks. As I was suffering from depression at the time, I call this period the blue years of my life. I quite literally cried my eyes out for three months. I felt totally abandoned and felt that God had abandoned me too. Shortly after my marriage breakup I was invited to a prophetic meeting with a group of Christians from Harrogate. I was not in a good frame of mind throughout most of the meeting but then at the end of the meeting, they started giving prophetic words to everyone. Right at the end an attractive middle-aged woman with brown hair came up to me and said,

"God is going to bless you for your suffering and he is going to give you the gift of healing."

She then prayed over me and I remember at the time being quite literally dumbfounded. I was at the lowest point in my life and there was this lady speaking over me and saying that God was going to bless me and give me the gift of healing. That word proved to be a catalyst for me to start looking for work and to get my life back together again. I managed to get a part-time job not long afterwards and I started doing voluntary work at the Healing Rooms in Leeds. It was there I met a lady called Sharon, who interestingly enough had been at the same prophetic meeting with me and when I met her, she told me that she had witnessed that lady pray over me and she had seen an anointing come over me as she prayed. I cried out to God to help me that night in my bedroom and was given a prayer to say by the Holy Spirit. I desperately wanted not to be on anti-depressants anymore and I prayed the following prayer. "Lord Jesus, I repent of all my sins. Please forgive me of all my sins. Please cleanse me of all sin with your precious blood. I believe that you died on the cross and rose again on the third day. Lord Jesus, please come into my heart right now and fill me up with your Holy Spirit. I accept you as my Lord, God and Saviour. Amen." This prayer is often called the sinner's prayer in Christian circles but I didn't have a copy of it in the house and I did not look it up on the internet. I simply repeated what the Holy Spirit gave me to say. That very night I received a dream about getting baptised in water. So, I drove to a local farm in Yorkshire called Hollybush where they have had Christian meetings for decades and I asked to be baptised in the river there. They very kindly agreed to my request and it was there that I really committed my life to Jesus. I was baptised in the river Rye on 8th August 2014.

This was not just a sprinkling of water on the head as I had experienced as a baby. It was full immersion as in the days of John the Baptist and was a very magical day for me. It seemed like I had left behind my unhappy childhood and failed marriage and that it was all at the bottom of the river. I felt washed clean spiritually that day, that Jesus had literally taken all my sins and failures away and nailed them to the cross. Glorious Day!!!! Although I had been a Christian since my confirmation, I was now a born-again Christian. Smith Wigglesworth hits the nail on the head when he wrote,

`To be saved is wonderful; to be a new creature to have passed from death to life, to have the witness of the Spirit that you are born of God – all this is unspeakably precious.

I experienced not just a physical cleansing in the water that day but also more importantly a spiritual cleansing where all your past sins are taken away and you become a new creation in Christ. All my depression lifted and I felt happy again for the first time in a very, very long time.

Not content with being baptised in water I decided I wanted more, I wanted to be baptised in the Holy Spirit as I had heard other Christians talking about being able to pray in tongues or in the Spirit. I decided that if I was going to do this properly there would be no half-measures. So, I drove down to Shrewsbury in February 2016 and I went on a Christian weekend where there was a group of born-again Christians and one of them prayed for me to be baptised in the holy spirit and receive the gift of tongues which is a heavenly language given by God. I did not receive it straight away as I refused to open my mouth which was needed in order for the tongues to be released, but a week after that it came spontaneously when I was driving in my car listening to worship music. I was simply overjoyed when this happened as I had grown up in the Church of England where the baptism of the Holy Spirit is quite often overlooked and preached on infrequently. I had been confirmed at the age of 15 but at no point had I been encouraged to seek the baptism of the Holy Spirit and the gift of tongues. Jesus however desires very much for us to have this gift as it gives you courage and boldness to witness and to pray for healing or deliverance for others. Smith Wigglesworth writes very well on this subject that when we are saved, we have the well of salvation bubbling up inside us but we need to go on further and seek the baptism of the Holy Spirit, and then from within us will flow "rivers of living water". Jesus showed us very plainly that if we believe in Him from within us will flow these 'rivers of living water`. He wants us to be filled with the Holy Spirit and to receive the gift of praying in tongues, or in the Spirit as it is often referred to as that is the evidence that we have received the baptism. I believed when I was a child that this gift was only for nuns or priests but that is not the case. It is available to everyone. All we have to do is repent, believe in our hearts that Jesus died and rose again on the third day from the dead and then confess Him as our Lord and Saviour. Next all that is needed is to seek the baptism of the Holy Spirit as it is given for the profit of ALL, male and female, Jews and Gentiles, church leaders and lay men and women. Even children can receive it.

For two thousand years, the mainstream churches have brilliantly preached on the saving power of the cross, on repentance and salvation but Jesus wants us to go further. The full gospel is not just repentance and salvation but also healing and deliverance. He wants us to seek the baptism of the Holy Spirit because then we are literally set on fire for Christ like his apostles were and we are then anointed and given DUNAMIS power to go out and witness, and pray for healing for the sick, and deliver the oppressed, the addicted and the mentally ill. Dunamis is the Greek word for power. Every single human being alive carries the Holy Spirit and we are literally made in the image of God down to our very cells. Our cells are bound together by laminin which if you look under a microscope is formed in the shape of the cross. Once we have the baptism of the Holy Spirit the dunamis power of God can literally flow through us so that we can help others just as the apostles did and this applies to the lay men and women in the church, as well as church leaders. It is like flicking an electrical switch in your house which is off to on, or the difference between driving your car in the lowest gear to putting your foot down and driving in top gear. All we need to do is seek the baptism of water and then the baptism of the Holy Spirit and the rest will follow. There is a psychologist in America called Doctor Sizer who started out as a brilliant Catholic priest. He graduated with a First-class honours degree and was a very dedicated priest but he never saw anyone healed or delivered from demons or baptised in the Holy Spirit and couldn't understand why. One night he was so hungry for God that he got down on his knees, repented of all his past sins and asked Jesus to come into his heart. Not long after that, he was baptised in the Holy Spirit by a group of Christians who met in the basement of his house when his life was changed forever. They prayed for him and he was literally lit up with the Holy Spirit from head to foot.

'Three people prayed with me. Their prayer asked Jesus to send the Holy Spirit upon me. Then they prayed in tongues, their own prayer language asking him to baptize me in the Holy Spirit. My body began to shake. I shook and shook more as convulsions of power overcame my body. I shook off the seat of the front pew of the church…. Power went through me in waves of electricity. The electricity went through me as I bounced off the floor time and time again. This went on for thirty minutes to an hour. I don't know exactly the time. As I got more used to the electrical impulses, I noticed they were accompanied by feelings of love. It was like liquid love pulsating through my entire being, penetrating even to my heart and my deepest recesses.' [1]

---

[1] Power Encounters by Dr Francis Sizer p21

Father Sizer's life was never the same from that moment on. When he prayed for people, they were healed and eight-year-old children were slain in the spirit when he gave a blessing over them. He then started a famous healing ministry in America. My life too changed irrevocably on 8th August 2014 when I was baptised in water and later in February 2016 once I received the gift of tongues. This is what Jesus meant when he said it is important to be born of water and of the spirit to Nicodemus. I was now born again and set on fire for Jesus. The reluctant disciple was gone forever.

Chapter 4

Out on the Streets – First Healings

One week after I received the gift of tongues, I went to my little village church as usual on a Sunday morning in a very contemplative frame of mind pondering on my weekend in Shrewsbury. I remember that day I had terrible hay fever that morning and I literally was streaming, my eyes and nose were running and I couldn't stop sneezing which was extremely embarrassing. What was even worse was I had left my tissues behind. Wondering what to do, I was just about to leave the service to go home and get some tissues when a nice lady behind me noticed I was struggling and gave me some tissues. I was extremely grateful to this lady as you can imagine and watched her intently as she walked up to the aisle with a walking stick. I noticed that she was grimacing and looked like she was in pain.

At the end of the service, I walked up to this lady who I will call Elizabeth. I asked her why she needed a walking stick, and whether she was suffering from arthritis in her legs and told her I was interested as I was working as a community carer at the time. She replied that the problem was actually her back. She was suffering from osteoarthritis, which was badly damaging the vertebrae and discs in her lower spine and she was indeed in a lot of pain. It was then that the strangest sensation came over me. I suddenly out of nowhere received a very strong urge to pray for this lady, it was simply overwhelming. So, I said rather nervously to Elizabeth, as I had never prayed for healing for anyone else at that point apart from my family,

"Would you like me to pray for you? Shall we see if we can get your pain levels down a bit?"

I fully expected her to refuse my request as this was the Church of England and it was simply not the done thing for a lay person to pray for another member of the congregation. To my great surprise, she accepted my offer. So, I took her outside and we sat down on the bench outside the church. I then put my hand on the base of her spine and commanded all the pain to go in the name of Jesus. I bound the spirit of osteo-arthritis and commanded that to leave her back, and then I prayed for all her vertebrae and discs to be totally healed and restored and to go back into place. I only prayed for her back as she did not ask me to pray for her knees or legs. I then prayed in tongues over her back for about a minute. After that, she stood up and said to me that all the pain had gone and she felt much better. So much better she ran into the church and announced to the interim priest that day that I had just prayed for her, that her back was healed and all the pain had gone. The priest looked at me and proceeded to tell me off telling me not to pray for anyone again, as he assured me that next time it would not work and they would not be healed. I went home feeling not surprisingly rather crestfallen. Every night I prayed to God and asked him for another sign that Elizabeth had indeed been healed and that it had not actually all been a figment of my imagination. I went back to church the following Sunday and Elizabeth came up to me to thank me at the end of the service. She told me that all her pain had completely gone from her back and that she was thrilled. Then she gave me the sign that I have been praying for all week. She said to me,

"Victoria, I didn't want to tell you at the time but when you were praying for me your hand felt hot. I could feel the heat coming from your hands!"

Heat of course, is a sign that the Holy Spirit is flowing so I was delighted as I knew that she had indeed been healed by Jesus the previous Sunday.

From that moment I decided to go out evangelising every week but I needed someone to go out evangelising with. My friends were all conservative Christians and would never have dreamed of doing such a thing so I prayed that God would send me someone to go out evangelising with as I always had a day off every week. A couple of weeks later a Christian called Christa called me, I had met her on the Shrewsbury weekend and we had exchanged phone numbers. She was on her way driving from London to Newcastle and wondered if she could stop and have a coffee and do some evangelising on the way home. I, of course, was ecstatic and I asked her where would she like to go. She suggested that we meet near York hospital, and as York Hospital is a large place we arranged to meet at the main doors. We never managed to even go for a coffee as just after greeting Christa, a man who had just had his toe amputated came out of the door pushed by his son obviously longing for a cigarette. We said hello to them both and offered to pray for the father as he was in a lot of pain. After we had done that his son asked us to pray for him as he had just snapped the cruciate ligament in his right knee. He was unable to play any sport and was awaiting surgery to reattach his ligament. Christa and I accepted his request and Christa put her hand on his shoulder, whilst I as this was quite a serious injury knelt down and put both my hands right around his knee front and back. I prayed for all the pain to go, and for his cruciate ligament to be totally healed and restored in the name of Jesus and to go back into the correct place. Then both Christa and I prayed in tongues for about a minute over his knee. A minute later he stood up and bent his knee in half and held it there, which you can't do with a broken cruciate ligament. He then exclaimed very loudly,

"I don't believe it. My knee is healed. I don't need the operation anymore. I am going straight back to church!"

I gave my phone number to his father as I wanted to know if his son was still feeling better that night. He rang me four hours later to say his son had rung him, his knee was totally healed and his son was over the moon. The funniest thing was that there was a lady laughing her socks off at Christa and me standing behind us having a cigarette, who clearly thought that Christa and I were crazy. Rather amusingly, she completely stopped laughing at us when she saw the young man was healed and asked us to pray for her stomach as she had very bad IBS. Christa and I never made it to the coffee shop that afternoon, we were so excited. You see Jesus is the same yesterday, today and forever. He loves to heal the sick and is just waiting for us to step out and pray for healing for others. The way we pray though is crucial. Intercessory prayers that we are taught to pray in the church are of no use when someone is standing in front of you with a ripped cruciate ligament. Jesus taught his disciples to command healing in the name of Jesus, to command the body part to be healed and to always pray in the name of Jesus. We have to stand on the authority that Jesus Christ has given us, to know who we are in Christ and say "Cruciate ligament, be healed in the name of Jesus", as if you are speaking directly to the body part. Intercessory prayers are of course essential for praying for the sick when a loved one is in hospital but it is far more effective to actually put your hand on the part of the body that is sick and command healing in the name of Jesus. There needs to be a paradigm shift in the way in which we pray for the sick, to follow the way that Jesus taught his disciples which is to lay hands on the sick and command healing in the name of Jesus.

I was over the moon as you can imagine after my afternoon with Christa and was determined to go out witnessing every week after that. I had been rather nervous going out evangelising with Christa but all fear was gone now. My part-time job paled into insignificance. All I wanted to do was go out and evangelise when I had my day off so I started looking for someone local that I could evangelise with. It was then I suddenly remembered that when I had been on the Christian weekend in Shrewsbury I had been put taken out on the streets and shown how to evangelise by an evangelist called Oliver. I sent him a Facebook request and asked him if he would like to meet up and go out on the streets and evangelise once a week and to my great delight, he remembered me from the weekend in Shrewsbury six months earlier and agreed to my request.

Chapter 5

Getting Braver – Healing Using a Hankie

Oliver was a very tall man, over six foot, with brown hair and brown eyes and striking still even though he was in his early sixties. By the time I met him he was divorced like me and was retired so he had plenty of time on his hands. The first time I met him he very kindly offered to buy me a sandwich in a café in York and we quickly made friends as we were both divorced and on our own and because we were both born-again Christians so we were not short of conversation. He also was a great evangelist and had been witnessing for years, whereas I was a beginner so I was thrilled to have found someone so experienced. I still remember our first afternoon in York together. We got chatting with a young homeless man who had recently been stabbed two weeks earlier. He had been stitched back up in casualty but he was still in immense pain. Oliver simply put his hand on the young man's back and prayed for all the pain to go and for all his muscles, ligaments and tendons in his back to be totally healed and restored. Then both Oliver and I both started praying in tongues over the young man. Very excitedly, he told me that the pain had gone right down and that he felt much better, whereupon we gave him a gospel tract and said goodbye.

After such an encouraging start Oliver said we should go out every week after that and we had lots of conversations with many homeless people. Often, we would buy them tea or coffee or buy them a sandwich. We very much concentrated on the homeless people but then after a month, Oliver said to me that we should be braver and offer to pray for others too who were not homeless. One afternoon at the end of August we were out in York witnessing and we came across a middle-aged lady who was sitting outside the Minster. She looked very out of breath and could not walk without a walking stick in spite of being relatively young. We got chatting with Sarah and her husband and she confirmed to Oliver and me that she did suffer from COPD and was very frequently struggling for breath so Oliver and I offered to pray for her. I put my hand just below her neck and Oliver put his hand on her shoulder. Sarah then spoke to us and said she had just had the most wonderful vision. She told us that as soon as we laid our hands on her and started praying that she could see a white star in front of her eyes. We carried on praying and she said she could feel heat in her lungs and in her back. We told her that was the Holy Spirit flowing and she said her breathing felt a lot better. So, we again left her with a gospel tract and said our goodbyes. After that, we met a group of homeless, one of which was a woman who had a drinking problem. I went off to buy her a sandwich and a cup of tea and left Oliver praying for her healing from depression. When I came back, she said she wanted to accept Jesus into her life so we led her through the sinner's prayer. The gospel of Jesus Christ is very powerful. It has the ability to lift depression, and bring joy and peace. All mine had gone after I became a born-again Christian and it was so lovely to see this lady happy and smiling, instead of depressed and miserable after we had shared the gospel with her. We had a very happy summer that summer witnessing in York and one day in August when it was very hot Oliver and I walked from Hunmanby Gap to Scarborough witnessing and praying for anyone that was struggling to walk with arthritic knees. To our great surprise, no one refused to let us pray for them and most were delighted.

I started to get braver and pray for people on my own if any of my friends needed prayer. I remember in August 2016 I was on Skype praying with a friend that I had prayed with for two years and he told me that he had been stung by a bee. His ankle had swollen right up and he had been to the doctor to get antibiotics as he was allergic to bee stings. He told me he was in a lot of pain. I offered to pray for his ankle and I prayed for all the swelling to go down and all the pain to go in the name of Jesus. At nine o'clock the next morning he rang me to say he was feeling better, all the swelling and the pain had gone by the time he went to bed the night before. He never took the antibiotics as he didn't need them. I am not taking the credit for any of these healings incidentally, our job as Christians is to pray but it is Jesus that does the healing. He is the same, yesterday, today and forever and he loves to heal the sick as it gives glory to God the Father.

Another time I was on Skype a Canadian man who I was praying with who I shall call Jimmy told me that he wasn't at all well and was receiving treatment for prostate cancer. I didn't know how to help this poor man but I then had a light bulb moment as I remembered how it says in the bible that many people were healed when they gave articles of clothing and hankies to Paul for him to bless. I, therefore, took a real step of faith and went out and bought some white hankies. I was on the ministry team at Leeds

Healing Rooms at the time which was a place for people to go for ministry and prayer if they were sick and needed help. I took my white hankie in and all the other team members prayed with me over the hankie and asked Jesus to fill it with the Holy Spirit. I then anointed it with oil in the shape of a cross and mailed it to Canada to Jimmy. Two months later I asked Jimmy how he was, and if he was feeling any better. To my great astonishment he replied that all the cancer was gone, he was completely healed and that he had sent my hankie to his best friend who had also been healed of lung cancer. In fact, a year later I was asked by a friend who lives in Harrogate to pray over a hankie and send it to a relative of hers with depression. This time I prayed on my own for the Holy Spirit to fill the hankie and I anointed it with oil. She was healed of depression and came back to her faith once she realised that God had healed her. These are very special healing miracles and show the immense power of God that if we step out boldly in faith, there are no limits to what the Holy Spirit can do. Jesus is able to do exceedingly above all that we ask or think according to the Holy Spirit that flows through us if we are dedicated Christians who pray and read the word daily. After all, our bodies are temples of the Holy Spirit. The stories that I have mentioned above are all stories of healing but Jesus is also able to do immense miracles which are called creative miracles. This is when Jesus gives people new body parts or heals broken bones, as he has a room full of new body parts in heaven ready and waiting.

Chapter 6

Creative Miracles – Club Foot Straightens and New Kidney

A creative miracle is as I have mentioned in my last chapter when Jesus does an absolutely astounding miracle and gives someone a new body part such as a new kidney or when someone has a broken arm and leg and needs surgery and the power of God falls on them and their broken bones are healed by the power of God. When I was a girl at school, I was taught that these miracles did not happen anymore and that indeed they stopped occurring after the death of the apostles two thousand years ago. I obviously had never seen a creative miracle in my life as it certainly had never happened in any of the Church of England services I had attended, but I have always longed to see one happen in front of my eyes. It was only a month after I had started going out on the streets witnessing that my wish came true. On 22 September 2016, I saw a man with a crippled leg and a club foot leaning on his car close to Bettys who I shall call Derrick. He was trying to get his wheelchair out of his car but obviously couldn't do it by himself as he was disabled. So, I stopped and offered to give him a hand and I picked up his wheelchair and opened it up for Derrick as he was clearly struggling. I then was about to say "Goodbye" when Oliver suddenly offered to pray for his ankle and foot as he had a club foot as well as a withered leg. I was not happy with Oliver as I had never prayed for someone disabled and wasn't sure if I had the faith to do it. Derrick however was very happy and accepted Oliver's request but asked if we could pray for him in Saint Helen's church nearby, rather than on the street. He also said to us,

"You have fifteen minutes only as I have to be at the bank for an appointment in twenty minutes."

At which point my heart started pounding very fast inside my chest as I had never prayed for someone with a club foot before and even worse, we only had fifteen minutes. Once inside the church, Oliver placed his hand on Derrick's shoulder and I placed my hand around Derrick's club foot and commanded the bones in his foot to line up and straighten in the name of Jesus and I commanded all the muscles, ligaments and tendons to be healed too. Oliver prayed in tongues for his shoulder and then both Oliver and I prayed in tongues for his club foot. It was then that the most amazing miracle happened in front of our eyes, his foot slowly straightened in two minutes. I didn't have time to pray for healing for his withered leg as Derrick said he had to go but the next morning he sent me a text saying his friend had come to dinner at his house, and couldn't understand how Derrick's foot was straight all of a sudden which was a medical impossibility as he had had umpteen operations on his ankle to try and straighten it. He texted me the next morning to say he had gone swimming and was able to walk on the bottom of the pool for the first time ever. Hallelujah!!!!

In November 2017, I was led to pray for two young girls sitting on a bench outside the Minster. One of them looked like she had been in a fight as she had a huge bruise on her forehead. They were friends and looked as if they were in their late teens, or possibly early twenties. I walked up to the girl with the bruise on her head asking her what had happened and her friend stated that her health was far worse because she had to go on dialysis at the hospital every week, as she had been born with kidney failure. The hospital had tried to give her a kidney transplant but the transplant failed soon afterwards. This was a golden opportunity for me to offer to pray for this young lady so I asked if I could pray for the young girl. I was not expecting her to be healed as she had two non-working kidneys but I said to the girl, "Let's have a go and see what God can do!" I then put my hand on the girl's back roughly where her kidneys were and Oliver put his hands on her shoulder. I started praying for both kidneys to come back to life again, to be completely healed and restored and for any pain to go. I also prayed that she would be able to go to the loo in the normal way once more. I had absolutely no idea if anything had happened but I gave her my phone number on a gospel card as I have never prayed for a new kidney before and was very keen to know if she was healed. Sure enough, four hours later her father rang me over the moon and told me that his daughter was healed as she had just gone to the loo for the first time in six years. Jesus had answered her prayer and given her a new kidney. Glorious day, I was overjoyed and so happy for this young girl and her father! I remembered that day the words that the prophetic lady had spoken over me several years earlier with awe and wonder, and regretted that I had doubted and not believed her at the time.

Oliver lived actually in a little village called Thorner near Leeds and was getting rather tired of driving into York each week and suggested that we went into Leeds occasionally. It was there that Jesus blessed us with two further creative miracles although they were years apart. On 27 November 2017, we decided to go to Leeds and we met a homeless man in Leeds market who was walking with a walking stick as he had a fractured ankle. He was also severely depressed and had a drink problem. I of course had grown up with a mother who had been an alcoholic so I immediately offered to pray for healing for his ankle and for his depression to go. I put my hands around his ankle and commanded his ankle to be completely healed in the name of Jesus and for all the pain to go, and for the bones in his ankle to go back into place. Oliver and I prayed fervently for this poor man and just as we were doing so, he exclaimed,

"I can see shafts of light coming down out of the corner of my eye!!"

Undaunted, we carried on praying and five minutes later he walked off jubilant, pain-free and without his walking stick as he didn't need it anymore. Oliver and I were as you can imagine totally ecstatic to see him healed and pain-free, and of course not depressed any longer.

In October 2019, we were again back in Leeds. By this time, we were witnessing in Knaresborough, York and Leeds but only once a week and Jesus blessed up with another creative miracle. I noticed a homeless man who was sitting outside Tesco's on the high street in Leeds and I walked up to him and started chatting. I noticed once I was up close, which I had not noticed initially as he was sitting cross-legged on the pavement, that he had a black splint on his left wrist. Christopher was homeless and had fallen and broken his wrist one night when he was drunk and was feeling very miserable as it was cold, his wrist was hurting and he had been put on a long waiting list for surgery. I was filled with compassion for Christopher as he was homeless, and because it was cold, winter was coming and I knew he was in pain. I offered to pray for healing for his wrist which he accepted. Oliver actually was not with me as he had gone off to buy Christopher a sandwich and a cup of tea so I had to pray alone. I put my hand on his wrist and commanded all the swelling to go down as he said it was all completely swollen under his plaster cast, I commanded all the pain to go in the name of Jesus and for all the broken bones to be healed and go back into place. Next, I commanded all his muscles, ligaments and tendons to be healed. Then he gave me a big grin and said to me: -

"My goodness, what have you done? You are a very powerful lady because the swelling has gone down and I can move my fingers and thumb again which I couldn't do five minutes ago!!"

I was careful to explain that Jesus had healed him not me and the interesting thing was that when I was praying for Christopher, a man came up and gave him £5. We left a considerably happier Christopher with a healed wrist, eating a ham and cheese sandwich, £5 richer and reading his gospel tract. I always left everyone with a gospel tract with the sinner's prayer on it, sometimes I would say it with them but more often than not they preferred to say it in private by themselves.

Chapter 7

Oliver's Tragic Illness and Death

Very sadly, which was a huge blow for me, Oliver was diagnosed with pancreatic cancer in the Autumn of 2019. He used to come to my house on Sundays and we would go to church together in Harrogate. In September he turned up to my house yellow, his face and neck were yellow and even his eyes were yellow. I had no medical training but even I knew that something was terribly wrong and I had enough knowledge to know that it was jaundice but I had no idea that it would be so serious. So, I said to Oliver,

"No Oliver, I am not going to church with you today because I am going to take you in my car and drive you straight to hospital."

I drove him straight to hospital in York and he was admitted and told that it was jaundice, and they kept him in for five days whilst they did tests on him. I went in every day as he told me he didn't want to worry his children and on the fifth day they operated and put a stent in. This was an absolute life saver and twenty-four hours later his jaundice was gone and he was well enough to go back home. What he didn't know but found out several months later when he was called to go for a check-up in Leeds was they had discovered cancer in his pancreas. I was very upset as Oliver was an absolute rock in my life, we evangelised every week together and had done for 3 years. At church, we prayed for Oliver to be healed, but to no avail. Over the space of a year, his health declined fast and it was hit and miss whether he was well enough to go out evangelising. I do remember that we went out to York with two other friends in January 2020 when we saw one last healing together. The four of us saw a man who I will call Stephen who was on a mobility scooter as he had a badly damaged spine and could barely walk. He was in immense pain all the time which was so bad that he was unable to work as a lorry driver anymore. This was obviously very serious for his wife and children as they very much needed him to be back working again. We asked him if we could pray for him and I put my hand on his neck and prayed for healing for his neck and spine in the name of Jesus, for all the damaged discs and vertebrae to be totally healed and restored and for all the pain to go. Oliver and my two Christian friends prayed for healing with me. We did not know if he was healed or not, but he swiftly got off his scooter and walked a few steps and said that his pain levels had gone right down and he felt better. The following week I bumped into him again in York and he told me that he could walk again, all the pain in his back was gone and he had applied to get a job again as a lorry driver. He never had the surgery on his spine. God is good. For a brief period, it seemed that Oliver was picking up but by October 2020 he was very weak and he died on 26 November 2020. I was very upset and couldn't understand why Jesus hadn't healed him when he had prayed for so many others to be healed, but then I understood that it was simply his time to go home. He had spent his life serving others and evangelising, and he had completed all that he was sent here to do. He had served the Lord faithfully in the short time that I had known him. His children rang me to tell me he had died on 26 November, on Thanksgiving Day at dawn. I prayed to Jesus fervently on the way to work that day, as I needed a sign that Oliver had gone to heaven, although I knew of course that he had. The Holy Spirit gave me psalm 100 which greatly reassured me. Oliver had entered the gates of heaven with thanksgiving and entered into the courts of heaven with praise.

Jesus knew that I still wanted to do ministry and another opportunity arose for me in the Spring of 2020 when I was asked to serve on the ministry team of an international ministry which was a tremendous opportunity for me. I was also asked in December 2019 to serve on the ministry team of a national up-and-coming ministry called the Filling Station both of which I accepted with alacrity.

.

Chapter 8

Zoom Ministry – In At the Deep End

During 2020 and 2021 both ministries were run on zoom due to the pandemic and every week several hundred people would log on from all over the world desperately wanting prayer for cancer, depression and mental illness, parents came with autistic children and people with marriage problems to the International Ministry. If you had asked me if it was possible for people to be healed through zoom pre-2020 I would have said it was impossible but we literally saw people being healed and touched by the Holy Spirit on a weekly basis on zoom. More than that my eyes were fully opened to the multi-faceted nature of the Holy Spirit, as we saw people receive the gift of tongues, and we also saw some people manifest demons on occasions which the Holy Spirit drove out of them. The International ministry has a large team of prayer helpers and I started off as a junior prayer helper as I needed to learn the ropes of how to do ministry on zoom but I progressed to be a senior prayer helper in charge of a breakout room. Every week I was able to pray for people for an hour sometimes even an hour and a half if we had twelve in a break out room as the numbers coming onto the zoom meeting were so huge. So, it was literally like being thrown in at the deep end, because every week we had to pray for healing, or for deliverance or for people to receive the gift of tongues. I very often felt like Peter must have felt when Jesus told him to step out of the boat and walk on the water. I remember vividly the first time I prayed for deliverance on zoom in July 2020. This was not the first time in my life I had prayed for deliverance as I had prayed for a gentleman who had come to us for help when I had worked in the Healing Rooms in Leeds who had been manifesting an evil spirit but that was at least three years earlier. An Indian Pentecostal priest came into the breakout room I was in. I of course was working as the Junior Prayer helper but the Senior helper I was working with at the time kindly let me pray first for Nigel. Nigel told me that he was getting angry all the time and shouting at his family, and therefore his relationship with his wife and children was being badly affected. He also told me that his finances were under immense strain due to the lockdown which also was making him angry and upset. Also, he was suffering from a urinary tract infection at the time too. I started praying and asked the Holy Spirit to come and touch Nigel. It was quite mindboggling really; I was praying on zoom in England to Nigel who was halfway around the world in India. I started to pray hard commanding the spirit of anger to leave him in the name of Jesus Christ, and for all fear and anxiety to leave him too. Then I prayed for the urine infection to leave him and for his bladder to be completely healed and restored. Lastly, I prayed for Jesus to bless his finances and for financial prosperity so that he would have enough money to provide for his wife and his children. As I was praying the Holy Spirit came down on him and he started coughing out all the anger, fear and anxiety. He was coughing for about three minutes. After that, we prayed in tongues over him and prayed that the Holy Spirit would fill him back up and for him to be filled with joy and the peace of the Lord. A week later he sent a testimony saying that all his anger was gone, his marriage was restored and he was completely better. I have contacted Pastor Nigel in India and he has given permission for me to share his testimony and his name in this book. This is his testimony: -

TESTIMONY FROM MINISTRY ROOM JULY 4TH

I thank God for helping me to attend the zoom conference on 4th July 2020. However, I joined the prayer room. I waited my turn. I was having a spirit of anger. Due to which my relationship with my wife and children got strained. I was also facing urinary issues. Also, financial issues in the family. When the sister prayed for me, I coughed many times rapidly. I felt very much release in my spirit and also in my body. The other sister also prayed for me and said in anger do not sin. I thank God that these prayerful ladies ministered to me and God used them to deliver me from the satanic oppression. I believe God is restoring my marriage, health and also the financial part. I am very much debited to this ministry for touching me and my family.

Thanks

Rev Nigel Lazarus.

That day Pastor Nigel was delivered from a spirit of anger which was causing havoc in his life. We often think that Christians can't carry evil spirits but that is not the case. I was at a Christian conference this year and prayed for a man who was an evangelist but before he became a Christian, he had been involved in glue sniffing. I started praying for him and a very evil spirit of addiction started to manifest. He was literally retching in a bucket for half an hour. He was completely delivered by the Holy Spirit half an hour later and was overwhelmed by what Jesus had just done for him. I have prayed for many people on zoom who have needed deliverance from pornography. I have learnt over the last two years how essential it is to lead a holy life because if you don't demons can enter your body. Fornication, Adultery, pornography, drug and alcohol abuse, smoking heavily, yoga and meditation are all gateways that will allow demons to gain access. I remember praying for one particular man on zoom who came on complaining of pain all over his arms. I asked him if he was leading a holy life at the moment which he said he was. I then started praying to Jesus and got the word PORNOGRAPHY so I asked him if at any point in the last several years had he been watching pornographic material, to which he confessed he had. I then prayed for him to be set free from an addiction to pornography and immediately all the pain left his arms. It is so important to watch what comes in through our eyes by watching clean films on the television and in the cinema as the eyes are the gateway to our souls. Yoga is the one which is most dangerous as is meditation as Christians tend to think they are safe which they are not. All the yoga poses are actually poses to worship Hindu Gods and are therefore demonic. Meditation also is harmful to Christians, and not recommended as its roots are in Buddhism and it is definitely not Christian. Jesus made it very clear that Christians should pray and worship God and not any other God as it is breaking the first commandment which is that we should have no other Gods apart from him. Jesus reaffirms this when he says to Thomas that he is the way, the truth and the life and that no one comes to the Father except through him.

I was at a conference in Peterborough this summer when a young woman called Imogen came up to me because she was in immense pain in her joints which was very strange as she was a young woman and definitely too young to have arthritis in her joints. I started praying for her and the Holy Spirit fell on her and she started hissing at me and manifesting a very evil spirit. The Holy Spirit told me this was a spirit of Yoga, which is associated with the Kundalini spirit and for a good fifteen minutes, I was commanding this evil Spirit to come out of her in the name of Jesus. She then proceeded to vomit in a bucket for 15 minutes as the Holy Spirit delivered her from all yoga and the Kundalini spirit. Finally, we prayed for her to be filled back up with the holy spirit and she left absolutely overjoyed because not only was she free of this evil spirit but also, she received the gift of praying in tongues. I nearly started crying as it was so overwhelming to see this young lady delivered in front of my eyes from an evil spirit and then filled up with the Holy Spirit and speaking in tongues in the space of half an hour. Both Imogen and I were simply overjoyed.

My most memorable zoom ministry took place in January 2022. A man from Bordeaux in France rang up the Filling Station and asked if he could receive prayer as he had bad pain in his shoulder and arm and was distressed as he was unable to do any sport. He was a young man in his thirties so this was deeply upsetting for him. As he was in France, Laura who heads up the local Filling

Station ministry asked him if he would like prayer over zoom and then Laura rang me and asked me to help. So, Sacha came on the call one cold night in the middle of January. Sacha told us that he was a lapsed Catholic and hadn't gone to church for many years to which I replied that in which case he would need to repent. I also told him that he needed to repent as that would increase his chances of being healed and I told him I really wanted him to leave the call completely healed and better. I also explained to him that Jesus was not the owner of a sweetie shop that gave out sweets for free, Jesus paid for all our sins on the cross.which meant we are able to receive salvation and healing but only through repentance of our sins and verbally confessing him as our Lord and Saviour. Then I asked Sacha if he would be willing to say the Sinner's prayer with me to which he agreed and he recited it perfectly line by line. After that both Laura and I asked the Holy Spirit to come down upon Sacha and completely heal his neck, arms and shoulders. At the end of the call, Sacha was very happy and read psalm 91 to us in French. Laura and I had no idea if he was healed or not but the next day he rang Laura full of the joys of spring and said he was over the moon as all the pain had left and he could do his sport and exercises again. He rang me too later on and told me that after we had both prayed for him, he had felt heat all over his body due to the Holy Spirit and he had to get in the shower!!! He told me he was so happy as he was able to do his exercises and go back to his sport which he loved. This was an important learning curve for Laura and me as we had never prayed together for anyone on zoom before but Jesus showed us that nothing is impossible for God.

It was not long before people started coming forward for prayer in the meetings as the physical Filling Station meetings opened up again in 2021. As soon as the meetings were back up and running again in person a middle-aged lady, I will call her Melanie came forward at the end of the meeting and told me that she was in real pain 18 months on from having contracted covid, that her lungs were hurting so much she felt extremely depressed. I offered to pray for her and asked the Holy Spirit to come down and heal her lungs of long covid. I commanded the coronavirus spirit to leave her lungs in the name of Jesus and we had to get a bucket as she started coughing badly for a good ten minutes. At the end she said she said her throat felt really tight so I read psalm 91 over her and the coughing immediately stopped and she was delivered. We then prayed for her to be filled up with the Holy Spirit. It is always important to do that because Jesus recommends it in the bible to stop any more spirits from coming back in. A week later she confided in me that the really bad pain in her lungs was gone, that she felt Jesus had healed her and she was thrilled to be able to lead a normal life again.

Interestingly enough only a month later, a young girl called Antonia came to one of the Filling Station meetings suffering from lumps in her mouth. She had started to feel ill after a recent vaccination, had not felt well ever since and was also suffering from anxiety. I started praying for healing for her and the same thing happened, she started coughing badly for about ten minutes and was delivered by the Holy Spirit. Then Laura came over and prayed for her in tongues to be filled with joy and peace. Antonia left in no doubt that she had just had a major deliverance by Jesus and texted me the next day to say she had slept for ten hours. I have heard from her since then and she is thrilled because the lumps in her mouth have all gone and the doctor has given her the all-clear. Jesus had completely delivered her and healed her, as he had done with Sacha and I do believe both were healed because they had humble and contrite hearts. God will not despise a broken and contrite heart that means more to him than any sacrifice or burnt offering. We have also had a man healed of vaccine damage. James came to one of the meetings looking grey and distinctly ill and the Holy Spirit told me he needed prayer. The following month I grabbed him and asked to pray for his healing which he accepted. I prayed for healing for him and he now looks completely well, has put weight on and the colour has come back into his face. Even better he stood up and testified that he was totally healed at the next meeting. Praise God! This shows that it is possible to be healed of vaccine damage and we have prayed for healing for several people from vaccine damage successfully through the filling station ministry.

The most extraordinary healing I have seen this year has to be of a middle-aged lady called Davina. She came to me in a Filling Station meeting wanting prayer for healing for herself, but also for her husband who was at home and not at the meeting who had serious digestive problems and was having stomach pains. I explained to Davina that we would have to pray by proxy for her husband as he was not there, so I asked her to put her hand on her stomach and started praying for her husband's stomach to be healed and for all his pain to go. The Holy Spirit obviously knew that Davina was standing in proxy for her husband as she started swaying badly and I had to grab another team member to catch her as she went down on the floor. She was slain in the spirit for five minutes with the Holy Spirit all over her. The next month she came back to the meeting with a smiling husband. She obviously must have told him what had happened at the last meeting.

Chapter 9

Freedom from Addiction and Generational Curses

Another area of deliverance that is extremely prevalent in modern society is the addiction to smoking, alcohol or drugs. So many are so oppressed by their addictions and have absolutely no idea that if they only sought out prayer, Jesus can heal them of their addictions. Chasing the Dragon written by Jackie Pullinger is a brilliant book where she tells her story of how she prayed for many Chinese men and women who were addicted to hard drugs. Those who came to Jackie were prayed over in the Spirit whilst they slept at night and were completely healed remarkably quickly without having to go anywhere near a rehab centre. My mother had been an alcoholic and had had to go into a rehab clinic when I was very young so I have been personally affected by this as I didn't see my mother for a year while she was drying out. We have had people come to the Filling Station who are addicted to cigarettes. Last year the Filling Station was contacted by a middle-aged lady called Annabel who was smoking two packets of cigarettes a day. It was ruining her health and costing her a lot of money. She seemed rather breathless as a result and did not have a car so Laura and I ended up driving to her house to pray for her. We had a lovely chat with Annabel over a cup of tea when she told us that she was worried there were generational curses in her family so we told her that we would definitely pray for all generational curses to be cut off her family line too, in addition to praying for her addiction to cigarettes to go. She was correct to tell us because if there are family members who are involved in the occult or in Freemasonry it can cause sickness and ill health in their offspring. As usual, we prayed for the Holy Spirit to come down and touch Annabel, we prayed that all generational curses would be broken off her and her family line by the blood of Jesus Christ and we bound the spirit of addiction and commanded her lungs to be healed and restored in the name of Jesus. Then we said our goodbyes and made our way home. A month later Annabel came to the meeting and joyfully told everyone that she had managed to stop smoking completely and said that she was feeling much better. Hallelujah!!!

Annabel was very fortunate as she did not exhibit any signs that she needed full-blown deliverance ministry, as can often be the case if you are a child of parents who have been involved in the occult or Freemasonry. Both of these can cause generational curses on offspring even if the offspring have become Christians in adult life. I prayed for a young woman on zoom last year who was very ill with Fibromyalgia, and had been for years because her mother had been dabbling in the occult. I led her in a prayer to repent on behalf of her ancestors for their involvement in the occult and I asked Jesus to wash her and her entire family line with his precious blood. I then commanded the spirit of fibro-myalgia to leave her in the name of Jesus and all other unclean spirits, particularly the spirit of witchcraft. At which point the Holy Spirit came upon her and she was literally retching in a bucket for ten minutes whilst all the unclean spirits were driven out of her. I then prayed for her to be filled back up with the Holy Spirit and she left the call very happy, set free and praising Jesus. It was the most moving thing I have ever seen in my life to see a young woman who was sick, healed by Jesus of fibromyalgia and set free from all generational curses. She left filled up with the Holy Spirit and speaking in tongues. All Glory to Jesus!

At the most recent Filling Station meeting in September, a young woman called Natalie came who also had an addiction to cigarettes in spite of being only young. That night everyone was supposed to pray over each other in groups of two or three but Natalie was desperate to give up smoking which I presume was costing her an awful lot of money, and she called me over to pray for her. I asked the Holy Spirit to come upon Natalie and then I started praying hard binding the spirit of addiction to cigarettes and commanding it to leave her in the name of Jesus. At which point Natalie started retching so we had to grab a bucket very fast to save the carpet. She was literally bent double retching in a bucket for 10 minutes. Once she was delivered, I then prayed for Natalie to be filled with peace and joy. By this time Natalie had her head up smiling with her arms wide open and was speaking in tongues. What a transformation!!!! What a wonderful God we serve, Natalie was healed of her addiction to cigarettes that night.

The last point I would like to make is if I know I am going to pray for deliverance, I make a point of fasting and in fact, I generally fast once a week because it glorifies God.

Every fast whether it is a strict fast of bread and water, or simply skipping one meal a day is a precious treasure to God. It isn't the length of the fast that is important but the love and effort put into it. It is so powerful because you are allowing the spirit to overrule the flesh. Fasting is a very useful tool to use for deliverance as demons are only driven out by the power of God, and not by our own strength. It is also very important to give God all the glory, we pray but Jesus is the one who heals and delivers. Lastly, deliverance should not be attempted without training in this area. It is not for the faint-hearted and it is of the utmost importance to put on the armour of God as mentioned in the book of Ephesians beforehand.

Chapter 10

Baptisms In The Holy Spirit On and Off Zoom

As I have tried to show in previous chapters, the Holy Spirit is multi-faceted and he knows what each person needs whether it is healing or deliverance from an evil spirit, or from something far more ordinary like anger or depression. He also knows when someone is desiring to be baptised with the Holy Spirit and receive the gift of tongues which is the evidence of being baptised in the Holy Spirit. I have prayed for many people to receive the gift of tongues on zoom in the last few years and they have all received it more often than not. I do believe that now however Jesus is pouring his Holy Spirit out in ways that we have never seen before, as I have personally witnessed four people hit with the Holy Spirit and baptised from head to foot in front of my eyes this year. One was on zoom on 7 May when I was praying for a South American man who had a history of mental illness. Once we had finished praying for healing for him, he told me that he would like the baptism of the Holy Spirit. Up until that point, all I had seen on zoom was that people would start speaking in tongues spontaneously but nothing more than that. This time was different. I started praying for him to be baptised in the Holy Spirit and he was looking at me expectantly with his hands open. I then started to pray in tongues over him. Then the most extraordinary thing happened I literally saw the Holy Spirit come down on him and his whole body started shaking to the extent that his cheeks were going in and out spontaneously. It was like there was a wind blowing around him which of course there was, a Holy Spirit wind. It lasted for about 3 minutes and then died down. He was completely calm and peaceful throughout and then when it was over, he then asked me to pray for his mother!!!!

Last December I went to a Jesus Fields conference in Cwmbran in Wales and at the end of the first day, I had to find someone to pray with. I spied a very pretty woman with long blonde hair on the other side of the room and she waved back. She then came over to me. What I hadn't realised was that this lady had the gift of prophecy in spades. I still remember now what she said to me: -

"Victoria, God has given me a picture of you and he is training you up for battle. I can see a picture of you with a bow and arrow. He also says he wants to see you dance like you did when you were a little girl."

I was quite overwhelmed by this beautiful word and was speechless for about a minute which is quite unlike me. And then I remembered that I was supposed to pray for her so I said to her,

"Is there anything you would like? What would you like prayer for?"

She replied that she would like the baptism of the Holy Spirit which always makes me feel rather nervous. Anyway, I started praying, asking Jesus to baptise her with the Holy Spirit and to give her the desires of her heart. Next, I started praying in tongues over her and the next thing I knew was that her little finger started shaking and wouldn't stop. Then it was her whole hand. It soon spread to both hands and by the end of it, the Holy Spirit blasted her whole body for five minutes in waves. At the end she sank to her knees totally overwhelmed. I couldn't believe it. I had never seen anything like that in my life. God gave her what she had asked for and more.

I went to a Christian conference this summer in Scotland and two people asked me for the baptism of the Holy Spirit, which they both received. One was quite an elderly lady with grey hair, who asked for healing for various health issues that she had. The weirdest thing was that she never asked me for the baptism of the Holy Spirit, it just spontaneously happened. I was praying in tongues over her for her healing and then all of a sudden, the Holy Spirit showed up and her arms and legs started shaking uncontrollably for five minutes. She was shaking so much that she could have fallen off her chair, but fortunately she remained seated on her chair as I was not sure if I would have been able to catch her. At the same meeting, I prayed for healing for a man who suffered from epilepsy and in fact had just come out of hospital. The same thing happened. He never asked me for the baptism of the Holy Spirit, it just happened in front of our eyes. I was in actual fact praying for all the fear and anxiety to go as his epilepsy was causing him to be afraid and anxious. I started praying in the spirit for him and all of a sudden, the Holy Spirit hit him and his arms started shaking. He was completely silent with a big smile on his face as waves of the Holy Spirit washed over him for about five minutes. His wife was watching all of this and got so excited she said: -

"Pray for me. Pray for me!"

So, I did. It was a very busy night. When this happens, it is a great anointing from the Holy Spirit. He fills you with all the gifts of the Holy Spirit which I will go through in more detail in the next chapter. All these gifts come by FAITH; they cannot be bought. The sorcerer Simon tried to buy the baptism of the Holy Spirit but was firmly rebuked and put in his place by Peter, as the baptism is given by faith, to those with a repentant heart who are saved and seeking the Lord earnestly. The baptism of the Holy Spirit is therefore greatly to be desired. It is a special anointing from God which gives you dunamis power to witness, and to pray for healing or deliverance for others. It is for ALL BELIEVERS, male and female, of every denomination, not just for a few select Church leaders, which is what the Church has led us to believe for the last two thousand years.

Chapter 11

Gifts of the Holy Spirit

For those who are unsure what the gifts of the Holy Spirit are they are as follows: -

WISDOM: In the gift of wisdom, we see God at work in our lives and in the world. For the wise person, the wonders of nature, historical events, and the ups and downs of our lives take on a deeper meaning. The matters of judgement about the truth, and being able to see the whole image of God. We see God as our Father and other people with dignity. Lastly, being able to see God in everyone and everything everywhere.

This is not a gift to be despised, King Solomon asked for and was given this gift and was renowned for his wisdom.

KNOWLEDGE: With knowledge we comprehend how we need to live as a follower of Christ. A person with understanding is not confused by all the conflicting messages in our culture about the right way to live. The gift of knowledge perfects a person's speculative reason in the apprehension of truth. It is the gift whereby self-evident principles are known. There is much deception in modern day society so this is an invaluable gift to be able to discern truth from deception.

FAITH: With the gift of faith, we overcome our fear and are willing to take risks as a follower of Jesus Christ. A person with faith is willing to stand up for what is right in the sight of God, even if it means accepting rejection, verbal abuse, or even physical harm and death. The gift of faith allows people the firmness of mind that is required both in doing good and in enduring evil. It is the gift to trust God and inspire others to trust God no matter the conditions.

THE GIFT OF HEALING: The gift to use God`s healing power to cure a person who is ill, wounded or suffering.

THE GIFT OF MIRACLES: The gift to display signs and creative miracles that give credibility to God's Word and the Gospel message. This is a healing which involves the sudden appearance of something that did not exist previously, such as new body parts.

THE GIFT OF PROPHESY: The gift to declare a specific message from God to an individual or group from the Greek word Propheteia. It should always be encouraging and used to build up others, and not judgemental or belittling. I have given an example of an uplifting word of knowledge that was given to me. Sometimes this is very useful when going out evangelising. I was going out evangelising with Laura one afternoon and God told her to look for a man with grey hair, and blue eyes wearing aftershave. Half an hour later we spied a man with grey hair, blue eyes and wearing aftershave from New Zealand. Laura preached the Gospel to him and we led him through the sinner's prayer. He was brought to tears when Laura told him that God has shown her a picture of a man with grey hair, blue eyes and wearing aftershave!

THE GIFT OF DISCERNING OF SPIRITS: The gift to recognize whether or not something is truly from God or in accordance with righteousness, or whether something is demonic. This is an invaluable gift to have and is part of the Great Commission that Jesus gave his disciples. This is not to be confused with spiritualism and consulting mediums which is strictly forbidden for Christians as is tarot cards, oujia boards and any involvement in the occult.

THE GIFT OF TONGUES: The gift to communicate in an unknown language to God. Most of the time tongues is a heavenly or angelic language but occasionally, God can give the gift of communicating in a foreign language to those who speak that language. Praying in tongues is extremely powerful and absolutely essential if praying for healing or deliverance. It gives courage and boldness to preach the gospel and stirs up the other gifts, especially the gift of prophecy.

THE GIFT OF INTERPRETING TONGUES: This is the gift to interpret a message from God given in a public setting like a Church and translate it back into your language

THE GIFT OF ADMINISTRATION: The gift to keep things ordered and in agreement with God's principles.

THE GIFT OF HELPS: The gift of a desire and capacity to always help others and do whatever it takes to achieve a task.

I am also going to add here the gift of the fear of the Lord as it is biblical and I feel sadly lacking in modern society. We really need this gift. Previous generations had it in abundance in years gone by.

FEAR OF THE LORD: With the gift of the fear of the Lord we are aware of the glory and majesty of God. A person with wonder and awe knows that God is the perfection of all that we desire: perfect knowledge, perfect goodness, perfect power, and perfect love. This gift is described as a fear of separating oneself from God. It is like a filial fear, like a child's fear of offending his father, rather than a servile fear, that is a fear of punishment. Also known as knowing God is all-powerful. Fear of the Lord is the beginning of wisdom because it puts our mind-set in its correct location with respect to God: we are the finite, dependent creatures, and He is the infinite, all-powerful Creator.

There are also twelve fruits of the Holy Spirit which are charity or love, joy, peace, patience, kindness, goodness, long-suffering, gentleness, faith, modesty, self-control and chastity. All the gifts of the Holy Spirit are given to us by FAITH once we have repented, accepted his sacrifice on the cross for the forgiveness of our sins, and confessed him as Lord, God and Saviour. When we are baptised in the Holy Spirit the blood of Jesus sprinkles our hearts and mind from an evil conscience, and we are then allowed into the Holy of Holies and given access to these spiritual gifts from the throne room of heaven. Al Collins writes beautifully in his book 'The Way',

`When you become my sons and daughters you can partake of heaven's treasures. There is always an abundance in Heaven. I have so much to give. When you abandon yourself to me and allow me to direct you, you will have access to heaven. The gates of Heaven will open to you......I do not hide the keys to me. They are freely offered to all. Take a key and then use it on a door the door will open. Don't go back through the door. Move forward. Step onto where the path takes you. Look to me as I will lead your way. The path enters into Heaven. It enters into my throne room.'[2]

[2]The Way by God and Al Collins p.24

Chapter 12

Making Disciples – Baptisms in Water

My last testimony which I want to share is that of Ivan's, which I have his full permission to share. I met Ivan at a Filling Station meeting in May 2022, although we didn't meet properly the first time as I was busy praying at the front. He did witness me praying for healing and deliverance for the young woman I mentioned called Antonia. What I didn't know was that Ivan was rather depressed and broken as I had been eight years ago. He was separated from his wife, which had broken his heart and then on top of that his wife had died so he was suffering from grief as well as a broken heart. He did not come forward for ministry at our May meeting but was so overwhelmed at what he saw that he drove an hour to go to the Filling Station at the Lakes two weeks later where he said the sinner's prayer and received ministry from a member of the team there and from me. I then suggested to him that I thought it would really help him heal, as it had me, if he was baptised in a river. He had been brought up a Catholic but had not been a practising Christian for many years. To my rather stunned reply, he told me to organise it. So, I rang Laura and Rob, and told them that we had our first candidate for a water baptism. Fortunately, we knew a friend with a beautiful house right on the river up in the dales where we could do it and on the 4th of June, the day of the Queen`s Jubilee, we took Ivan up to be baptised in the river and his young daughter. It was such a beautiful day; the sun was shining overhead as Laura and Rob baptised Ivan in the river. The sun sparkled on the water as he was fully immersed, and came up again to the words:

"Die with Christ.… Rise with Christ".

Not many days after that he received the gift of tongues. We took a video of his baptism and looking back at it now, it is as if you can see the Holy Spirit fall on him as he came up out of the water. I have kept in touch with Ivan since that day, and he is literally a new man in Christ. Jesus has healed his broken heart, and he is happy once more. Not only that but he is on fire for Christ, baptised in the Holy Spirit and on his holiday to Croatia he was witnessing what God had done for him to his friends and family. Hallelujah!!!! He has returned to his first love, Jesus Christ, once more. Like me, all the hurt and grief was washed away and left at the bottom of the river, and he has emerged a new man radiant and filled with the living water of the Holy Ghost. Hallelujah!!! This is the importance of being baptised in water. It is not just a physical cleansing but a spiritual cleansing too as Ivan said a prayer of repentance before he went into the water. Then we are a clean vessel ready to receive the gift of the Holy Spirit. It is the model that John the Baptist used when he baptised people in the river for the forgiveness of sin. It is what Jesus is referring to when he said to Nicodemus you must be baptised in water and of the Spirit to enter heaven. Smith Wigglesworth wrote eloquently about the importance of holiness in order for the Holy Spirit to indwell,

"When we have the right attitude, faith becomes remarkably active. But it can never be remarkably active in a dead life. When sin is out, when the body is clean, and when the life is made right, then the Holy Spirit comes, and faith brings the evidence."[3]

As I have said before, Ivan can now pray in tongues so that is the evidence that he has received the baptism of

[3]Smith Wigglesworth Devotional p.286

the Holy Spirit. Due to Ivan's courage, we then had five more people who came forward for water baptism this September. I was very privileged to attend their baptism which took place at the same river. One of the women who was baptised wrote about her experience and has agreed to let me share it here:

`Coming up to my 54th birthday, I decided to do something special. I decided to make my commitment to God official and get baptised. But I didn't want to be baptised inside the physical walls of a church building, I wanted to be baptised outside. As ever, God was listening. Less than a month later, an opportunity to be baptised in the River Ure materialised.

We arrived at the farmhouse of a local churchgoer where she welcomed us to her property and directed us down a path into the woods. The path led to a campfire site where the four other baptism candidates and myself congregated with family, and friends. We warmed ourselves by the fire and joined in prayer before continuing down the path to the river.

One-by-one we repeated our vows on shore. As I renounced my sins, the importance of this special day kicked in. The silent commitments I had made to God over the years in prayer paled in comparison with this public commitment and declaration by the banks of the river.

With the sheltered woodland behind me, I looked across the river at the green pastures beyond. The setting was idyllic and emerging from the woods the baptism seemed like the perfect metaphor for "dying with Christ" and "walking in newness".

Both nervous and excited, I took the hand of a fellow churchgoer and stepped in the gently flowing river. He steadied me as we tread the rocky bottom to the middle of the river. I can't remember much of what was said to me in the river. To focus myself, I fixed my gaze on the woman speaking and whispered a silent prayer of gratitude to God. Then the church team immersed me and assisted me as I rose again.... `

I very much feel that God is doing a new thing and that he is pouring his Holy Spirit out on the world now as we are living right in the End Times just before the Great Tribulation starts. Everything that the bible has prophesied is coming to pass in front of our eyes. War and rumours of war are taking place with the bloody war between Russia and Ukraine which has every possibility of escalating into Europe. There is famine in many countries in the world and we have had a pandemic for the last three years, of which I could write a whole book about that alone, but this is not the place for it. The one world religion and one world order are rising fast, in fact last September Pope Francis signed an agreement in Kazakhstan ratifying the One World Religion at the 7th Congress of World and Traditional Religions. There is much darkness and evil in our world is rising faster than ever. However, God is still in control and he has another plan. What the devil planned to kill, steal and destroy in the form of the pandemic God is using to bring people back to him. I believe there will be revival and huge numbers of people are coming back to Christ because of the pandemic. I am convinced that we will see more and more baptisms at the Filling Station as people are hungry for God and want answers. Many are waking up and realising that actually what is going on in our world today is a very fierce battle between God and the Devil. God is raising up his own army now, a remnant army, those who are born again and baptised in the Holy Spirit who are not afraid to step out in faith to pray for the sick and the oppressed. I believe that we are coming into a time of revival when we will see great miracles happen across the globe. God has not finished yet with England either. The death of Elizabeth Queen II on 8 September 2022 marked the end of an era, but I believe God has great plans for Britain. She will rise up out of the ashes and be a watchtower and shining light to the other nations. She was a great Christian nation and will be once more. We will see the Holy Spirit move if house churches are set up which allow for people to share testimonies and to pray for each other. Then we will see miracles, signs and wonders as they used to in the early church. The Happy Hunters had a famous healing ministry in the USA in the eighties and had a vision of the latter rains revival with miracles happening all over the globe through Christians who are lay men and women, like me. They saw the entire world covered in bands of silver and gold everywhere, from the mountains to the valleys.

'God is going to give to the world a demonstration in this last hour as the world has never known. These men and women are of all walks of life, degrees will mean nothing. I saw these workers as they were going over the face of the earth. When one would stumble and fall, another would come and pick him up. There was no 'big I' and 'little you,' but every mountain was brought low and every valley was exalted, and they seemed to have one thing in common – there was a divine love, a divine love that seemed to flow from these people as they worked and lived together. It was the most glorious sight that I have ever known. Jesus Christ was the theme of their life...As I watched from the very heaven itself, there were times when great deluges of this liquid light seemed to fall upon great congregations, and that congregation would lift their hands and seemingly praise God for hours and even days as the Spirit of God came upon them. God said, "I will pour my Spirit upon all flesh," and that is exactly what happened. And to every man and every woman that received this power, and the anointing of God, the miracles of God, there was no ending to it.'[4]

I am writing this book therefore to encourage lay men and women in their walk of faith, and I hope teenagers will read this book too. I have been a housewife for a large part of my life and I have never done a theology degree but God has used me in the last few years because he knows I am willing to step out in faith. All we need is to seek the baptism of the Holy Spirit and buckets of courage, which Jesus will give to those who have repented of their sins and confessed him as their Lord and Saviour. It is time for us to shake off the shackles of religion and know who we are in Christ, that we are temples of the Holy Spirit, and understand that we need to pray with the authority of Jesus Christ and walk in it. He is looking for humble hearts, those who are brave enough to step out of the boat and serve him. It is time to get off the fence and choose this day whom you will serve. Choose wisely, I choose Jesus as I know who wins this battle in the end.

[4] How to heal the sick Charles and Frances Hunter p13

Milton Keynes UK
Ingram Content Group UK Ltd.
UKHW051538100823
426660UK00013B/60